BARACK OBAMA
Son of Promise, Child of Hope

NIKKI GRIMES · ILLUSTRATED BY BRYAN COLLIER

Simon & Schuster Books for Young Readers

New York London Toronto Sydney New Delhi

ne day Hope stopped by for a visit.

It was early evening, and a boy named David sat on a tenement floor, glued to the TV.

"Who's that?" the boy asked his mother, pointing to the screen. His mother looked up from a frayed sofa and set her newspaper aside.

"That's Barack Obama," she said.

"Braco-what?"

"Barack Obama," she repeated with a smile. "I know it's a mouthful. Anyway, he's someone very special."

"Why?"

"Well, for one thing—"

"How come those people are shouting his name?"

"Because he—"

"Are they all his friends? They must be his friends. What's his name again?"

"Boy! You are about to wear me out!"

"Sorry," David whispered.

The mother patted a spot on the sofa beside her.

"Come," she said. "If you sit still, I'll tell you his story."

They used to call him Barry.
His family stretched
from Kansas to Kenya,
his mama, white as whipped cream,
his daddy, black as ink.
His mama's folks, Gramps and Toot,
were part of the first family
he ever knew.
Love was the bridge
that held them all together.

"I wish Grandma and Grandpa lived close by," said David.
"So do I," said his mother.

In Hawaii,
breathing in the scent
of ginger blossoms,
Barry grew—
swimming, surfing,
and spearfishing next to
playmates from places like
Portugal, China, India, and Japan—
and never once did he ask
if all those people
could get along.
They just did.

"Like the kids in my class!" said David.
"You're right," said his mother.

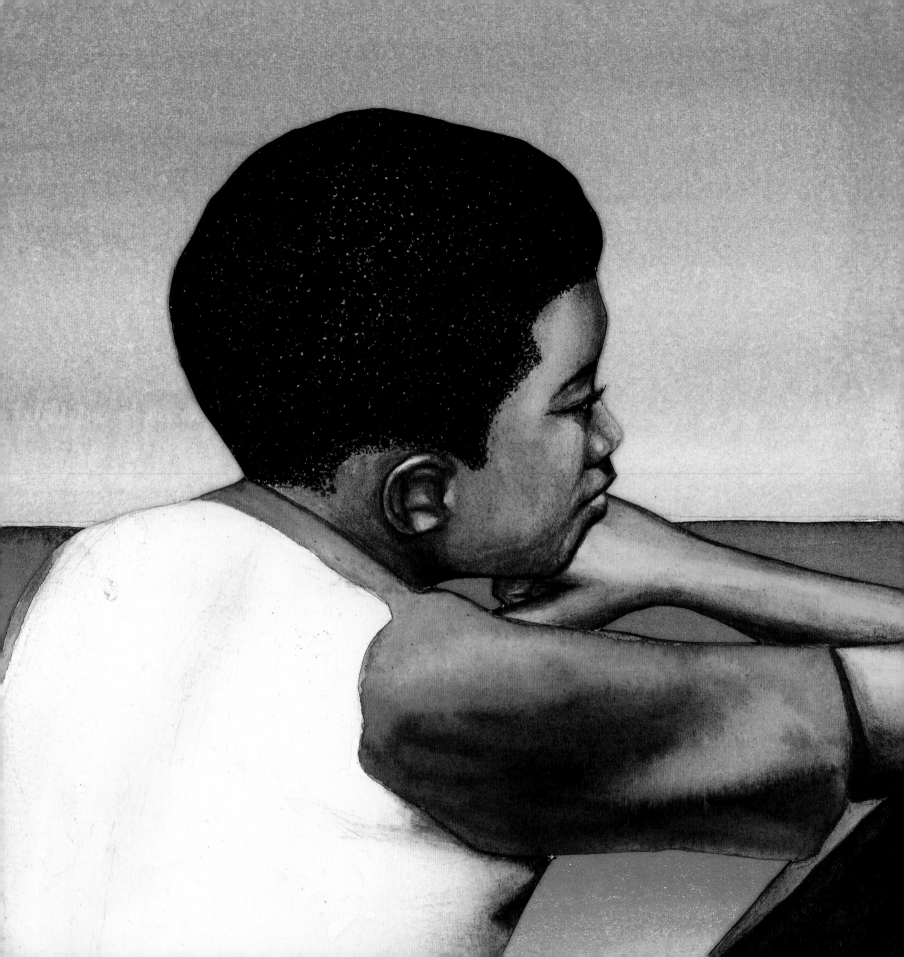

Honolulu looked like heaven.
But even though the blue of the sea
was sharp enough to slice the sun,
and the sun warmed the sand between his toes,
and the sand sparkled like diamonds,
nothing could fill the hole in Barry's heart
once his daddy went away.
His mom, and Gramps, and Toot
told him brave and funny tales of his father's past
to soothe his hurt and make him laugh.
But that didn't stop Barry
from feeling sad sometimes,
especially when he heard the word *Divorce*.

"I miss my dad too," said David.
"I know you do," said his mother.

Barry's mom married
a man named Lolo
and—Oh! The wonderland
he took Barry to: Indonesia,
a land of pet gibbons and pet crocodiles.
Barry laughed himself silly
sliding in the rainy-season mud.
He caught crickets, flew kites,
and joyed in the jungle
at the edge of his new home—
a perfect paradise, until
the sight of beggars
broke his heart.
Barry started to wonder,
Will I ever be able
to help people like these?
Hope hummed deep inside of him.
Someday, son.
Someday.

"There's lots of poor people, huh, Mama?"
"Yes, honey. I'm afraid so."
"Mama," said David, "we gotta help them."

Before dawn each morning
Barry rose, his mother's voice
driving him from dreamland.
Time for learning English grammar
and the Golden Rule.
"Be honest. Be kind. Be fair,"
she taught him.
"Your father is smart and strong
and full of courage.
And you will be just like him."
How can I? thought Barry.
I don't even remember his voice.

"I'm smart," said David. "I can spell S-C-H-O-O-L."
"Very good!" said his mother. "You keep that up!"

Back in Hawaii
a surprise came one day.
"I'm here, son," he heard his father say.
Barry listened to the strange song
of his father's voice.
"Your grandmama says
you are doing very well in school.
It's in the blood, I think."

Was this tall and skinny Harvard man
the one who lived in all those stories?
For a time all Barry could do was stare.
As the days passed,
they would share talks and walks.
And then, his dad was gone again,
a ghost once more.
Hold tight, said Hope.
This strand of memory
is stronger than you know.

"I wish I could meet my daddy," said David.
"I know, son. But no matter what, you've got me."

The sun and moon paraded past
Pali's peak more times than Barry's
quick mind could count.
Soon, he pounded across the high school gym
slamming the basketball his father
had sent him one Christmas.
A few letters flew back and forth
from mother to father,
from father to son.
Barry was the bridge
that connected them.
Sadly, some days
he felt as if that bridge
were sinking.

"What's a Pali?" asked David.
"Pali is a mountain in Hawaii," said his mother.
"Oh."

"Who am I?" asked Barry.
"I don't look like my mother.
I don't look like my father.
I only look like me."
Barry was dizzy with questions.
"You are not your father,"
a friend told him.
"You are not your mother.
You must choose your own way."
Choose what? thought Barry.
Choose how?
He searched for courage
inside himself.
Hope was waiting there.

"What is hope, Mama?" asked David.
"Hope is believing in something before you see it."
"Like make-believe?" asked David.
"No, honey," said his mother. "Hope is real."

Barry's mind spun like a top.
How could he know
which way to go?
Listen, said Hope. And he did.
There it was! The answer repeating
like a chorus in his ear:
"Education is the key," said Gramps.
"Education is the secret," said Toot.
"Education is the way," said Mom.
"Education is the path," said his father.
"Remember: It's in the blood."

"What do I have in my blood?" asked David.
"A kind heart, and a good brain—just like Barry."

Barry rolled up his sleeves and studied
in the shadow of Pali's peak,
in the shadow of the Hollywood sign,
in the shadow of Langston's Harlem.
Still, he couldn't stop asking,
"Who am I?"
Some called him an ugly name
too terrible to repeat,
but he refused to answer to that.
Instead, one morning
he slipped on the name
he'd been born with,
the name of his father: Barack.
For the first time in his life,
he wore it proudly,
like a coat of many colors.

"Like Joseph in the Bible!" said David.
"You remembered!" said his mother.

When Barack wasn't studying,
he liked to jog along the Hudson River.
He couldn't help but notice
the river of hurt and hate and history
that separated blacks and whites.
Being both, he could not take sides.
Don't worry, said Hope.
I will be your bridge.
In time, you will be the bridge
for others.

David's mother sighed. "Barry's aunt called him at school because his daddy died."
"I'll bet he cried," said David.

Barack hid his sadness.
Study, said the voices of his childhood.
Watch. Learn. Keep your eyes open.
Barack's eyes saw
the hungry and the homeless,
crying out like beggars in Djakarta,
burning a hole in his heart.
When his classes came to an end,
he raced to Chicago
to join hands with the church,
to learn new lessons:
not how to be black or white,
but how to be a healer,
how to change things,
how to make a difference
in the world.

"Hurray!" said David.
His mother gave him a squeeze.

The work was grueling,
with stretches of failure,
and puny patches of success.
Door-to-door Barack went,
early mornings, late nights,
pleading and preaching,
coaxing strangers to march together,
to make life better for everyone.
He worked as hard as a farmer,
planting the words "Yes, we can!"
like seeds in spring.
Impatient, Barack kept wondering
if those seeds would ever sprout.
He worried that the hope in him
would fade away.

"He didn't give up, did he?" asked David.
"What do you think?" asked his mother.

One Sunday when Barack was sitting in church,
Barack heard God say, "Slow down.
Look around you.
Now look to me.
There is hope enough here
to last a lifetime."
Barack smiled,
tears rolling down his cheeks.
Suddenly he knew for certain
Hope would last long enough
for him to make a difference.

"Why did he cry, Mama?"
"They were happy tears, son. Happy tears."

Before Barack chased his future,
he visited his past,
traveling to Kenya
to find his family,
his father's bones,
and his own place
in the circle of Africa.
He sat with Auma and Zeituni,
Jane and Sarah, Yusuf and Sayid.
He swapped stories with Roy and Bernard,
Mark and George, and all the other relatives
who had prayed for such a day.

Finally, Barack knelt in the soil
at his father's grave,
listening to the still, small voice
that spoke to his heart:
Go now. Fly free.
Become the man
you were meant to be.
Live in hope.
Keep the past in memory,
but shape your own tomorrow.

"Tomorrow, tomorrow, tomorrow," said David.
"What's so great about tomorrow?"
"Well," said his mother, "if we have hope today, we
get to make tomorrow whatever we want it to be."

Hope may be slim and beautiful,
but she is no weak thing.
Barack proved that when he
    went to Harvard Law School,
    convinced people to join hands in Illinois,
    wrote new laws to give the poor a better chance.
He proved it again when
all of Washington, D.C., wondered
what this skinny kid
with the funny name
could offer a nation in need.
But the hope that lived in Barack
burned bright,
and on the night he became senator,
everybody felt the flame!

"Is that why everybody's shouting his name?"
"No, son. There's more to the story."

One star-kissed night four years later,
as his wife Michelle stood by,
Barack smiled on a sea of faces
from Wichita to Waikiki.
He saw whites and blacks, rich and poor,
Christians and Muslims and Jews;
he felt the presence of Gramps and Toot,
he saw the ghosts of his parents,
of Martin Luther King Jr. and JFK.
And on that special day
Barack was the bridge
that held them all together.
"Thank you for electing me president," he said.
"Can we make America better?
Can we work together, as one?"
With a single voice
the crowd called out,
"YES! WE CAN!"

The little boy sat silently for a while. Then he said, "Mama, I've been thinking. When I grow up, I want to be the president. Is that okay?"
His mother blinked back tears, crushed David to her chest, and held him there for a long, long time.

AUTHOR'S NOTE

On November 4, 2008, the popular Obama campaign mantra "Yes We Can" became "Yes We Did"! America elected its first African American president and the world will never be the same. How did it all happen?

The 2008 American presidential election was one of the most exciting our country has experienced since the Kennedy era. One of the reasons for that was "the skinny man with the funny name," Senator Barack Obama, the first African American candidate with a genuine chance of becoming president of the United States. I wasn't convinced of this until he won the all-important Iowa caucus.

Was Iowa a fluke? Some wondered that after Obama lost the next big contest, the New Hampshire primary. But later in the race, he went on to win eleven primaries and caucuses in a row! The air crackled with excitement, and day by day the excitement spread from coast to coast. In my own heart, I began to dare to hope that Obama might win the Democratic nomination for president.

As an African American born before the Voting Rights Act was signed in 1965, I honestly didn't know if I would live to see this day. I'm sure there are other African Americans who feel the same. But African Americans aren't the only people who supported Barack Obama. His cry for change stirred the hearts of whites and blacks; Asians and Latinos; Christians, Muslims, and Jews; rich and poor; young and old—Obama has made believers of them all.

On June 3, 2008, after seventeen hard months of campaigning against his chief rival, Senator Hillary Rodham Clinton, Barack Obama became the first African American to win a major party nomination for president of the United States.

From that moment forward, the world held its breath with nervous anticipation. Was America truly ready for an African American president? Would the spirits of slaves who helped to build the White House soon welcome a First Family of African descent into its hallowed halls? On November 4, 2008, America went to the polls to answer those questions, and the answer was a resounding "Yes."

What kind of president will Barack Obama prove to be? Only time will tell. One thing is certain: The world will be watching. Will you?

Nikki Grimes
Corona, California
November 5, 2008

ILLUSTRATOR'S NOTE

This picture book is a glimpse into the life history of President-elect Barack Obama, spanning from his early childhood to close to the present. Each page is created in watercolor and collage, which acts as a metaphor for piecing different parts or issues together to make something new, whole, or complete. This theme has been a constant thread running through Barack's life. Young Barack was raised by his mother and grandparents, who were white. He was also the son of an African father, who was absent most of Barack's life. Barack's journey toward manhood took him to different parts of the world, which gives him a unique perspective. You will see Barack Obama grow as the result of a deep search—his attempt to balance race, identity, and how to make the world better. The best part for me is how Barack Obama seeks and discovers answers to questions about hope, courage, and change. This book celebrates Barack's ability to piece life's issues together to create a courageous vision for the world.

Bryan Collier
Marlboro, New York
November 5, 2008

BIBLIOGRAPHY

Brill, Marlene Targ. *Barack Obama: Working to Make a Difference.* Minneapolis, MN: Millbrook Press, 2006.

Obama, Barack. *The Audacity of Hope.* New York: Three Rivers Press, 2006.

———. *Dreams from My Father.* New York: Three Rivers Press, 1995.

ADDITIONAL SOURCES

"About Barack Obama." Barack Obama: U.S. Senator for Illinois. http://obama.senate.gov/about/.

Developing Communities Projects, Inc. www.dcpincorp.org/index.html (accessed January 11, 2008).

"Interactive Family Tree." *Chicago Sun-Times.* http://www.suntimes.com/images/cds/special/family_tree.html.

"Meet Barack." Obama'08. www.barackobama.com/about/.

Obama, Barack. "Book Excerpt: Barack Obama." *Time,* October 15, 2006. www.time.com/time/magazine/article/0.9171.1546298.00.html.

Shiver, Kyle-Anne. "Obama's Alinsky Jujitsu." *American Thinker,* January 8, 2008. www.americanthinker.com/2008/01/obamas_alinsky_jujitsu.html.

Wikisource. s.v. "Author: Barack Obama." http://en.wikisource.org/wiki/Author:Barack_Obama (accessed January 11, 2008).

1961

On August 4, Barack Obama is born in Hawaii to Ann (Dunham) and Barack Obama. Kenyan-born Obama Sr., himself a Harvard grad, began life herding cattle on his father's farm. He and Ann met at college in Hawaii.

1967

Divorced from Obama's father, Obama's mother marries Indonesian Lolo Soetoro. The new family moves to Djakarta, where Barack attends a school taught in the Indonesian language. He still speaks Indonesian today.

1971

Obama returns to Hawaii and enrolls at Punahou School.

1979

Enters Occidental College in Los Angeles.

1981

Switches to Columbia University in New York.

1982

Obama's father dies.

1983

Obama graduates from Columbia with a degree in political science.

1985–88

Does organizing in Chicago; visits Kenya; enters Harvard Law School.

1990

Obama becomes the first African American president of the *Harvard Law Review.*

1991

Obama graduates from Harvard with honors.

1992

Becomes a civil rights attorney in Chicago. Barack and Michelle Obama are married by Rev. Jeremiah A. Wright Jr. at Trinity United Church of Christ, their home church in Chicago.

1995

Three Rivers Press publishes his memoir, *Dreams from My Father.* A few months later, his mother dies of ovarian cancer.

1996

Wins election for Illinois state senate, where he serves for seven years.

1999

Obama welcomes the birth of his first child, daughter Malia.

2000

Runs for U.S. representative from Illinois against Bobby Rush, but is trounced in the primary by a two-to-one vote.

2001

Obama's second daughter, Natasha, is born.

2004

Elected U.S. senator for Illinois. Addresses the Democratic Convention to wild applause.

2005

Receives NAACP Fight for Freedom Award and Chairman's Award.

2006

Three Rivers Press publishes Obama's *New York Times* bestseller *The Audacity of Hope.*

2007

On February 10, Obama announces his run for president.

JANUARY 2008

Obama wins the Iowa caucus and South Carolina primary. Between January and June, Obama wins primaries and caucuses in thirty-one more states and territories.

JUNE 2008

Obama claims the Democratic nomination for President.

NOVEMBER 3, 2008

Obama's grandmother, Madelyn Dunham, dies.

NOVEMBER 4, 2008

Barack Obama wins the election to become the 44th president of the United States.

JANUARY 2009

Obama is inaugurated as president.

FEBRUARY 2009

Delivers his first speech to joint session of Congress.

OCTOBER 2009

Named the winner of the 2009 Nobel Peace Prize.

APRIL 2011

Obama announces that he will seek reelection in the 2012 presidential election.

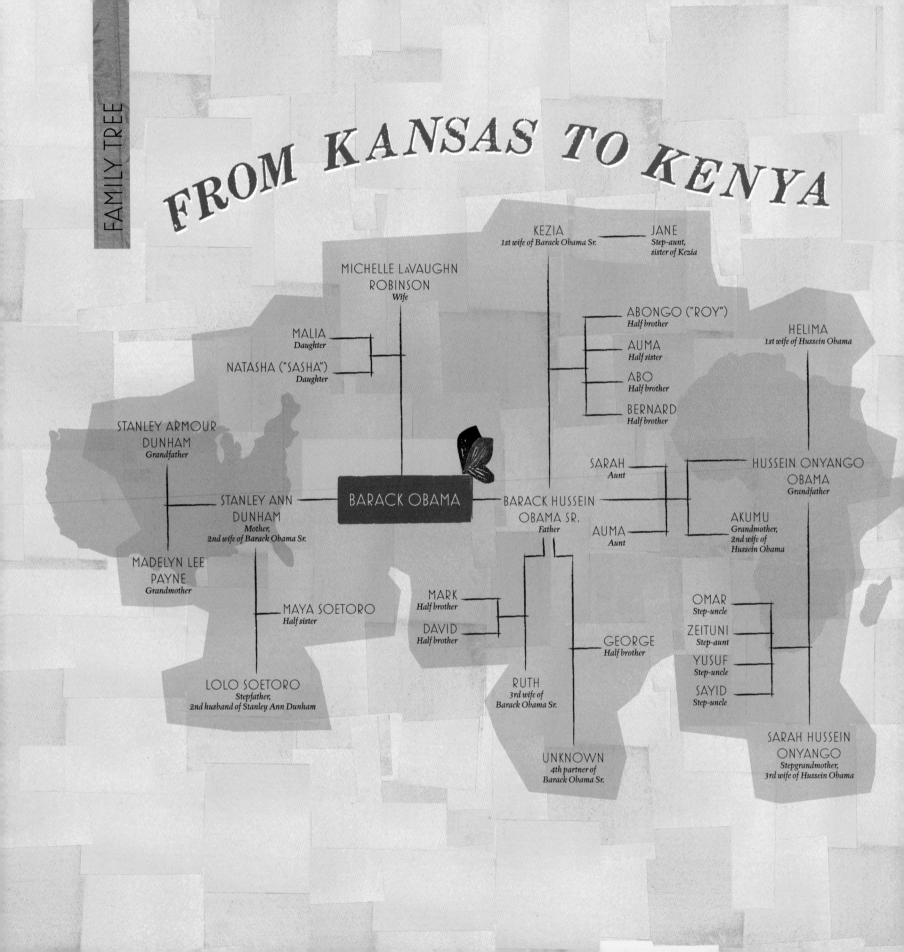

FROM KANSAS TO KENYA

KEZIA
1st wife of Barack Obama Sr.

JANE
*Step-aunt,
sister of Kezia*

MICHELLE LaVAUGHN
ROBINSON
Wife

ABONGO ("ROY")
Half brother

AUMA
Half sister

ABO
Half brother

BERNARD
Half brother

HELIMA
1st wife of Hussein Obama

MALIA
Daughter

NATASHA ("SASHA")
Daughter

STANLEY ARMOUR
DUNHAM
Grandfather

SARAH
Aunt

HUSSEIN ONYANGO
OBAMA
Grandfather

BARACK OBAMA

STANLEY ANN
DUNHAM
*Mother,
2nd wife of Barack Obama Sr.*

BARACK HUSSEIN
OBAMA SR.
Father

AKUMU
*Grandmother,
2nd wife of
Hussein Obama*

AUMA
Aunt

MADELYN LEE
PAYNE
Grandmother

MAYA SOETORO
Half sister

MARK
Half brother

DAVID
Half brother

OMAR
Step-uncle

ZEITUNI
Step-aunt

YUSUF
Step-uncle

GEORGE
Half brother

SAYID
Step-uncle

LOLO SOETORO
*Stepfather,
2nd husband of Stanley Ann Dunham*

RUTH
*3rd wife of
Barack Obama Sr.*

SARAH HUSSEIN
ONYANGO
*Stepgrandmother,
3rd wife of Hussein Obama*

UNKNOWN
*4th partner of
Barack Obama Sr.*

FOR EVERY AFRICAN AMERICAN BOY AND GIRL, WHO MAY NOW DREAM OF SOMEDAY BECOMING PRESIDENT. —N. G.

I HOPE THIS STORY INSPIRES YOU TO NEVER GIVE UP, TO CONTINUE TO SEEK ANSWERS TO YOUR OWN LIFE'S QUESTIONS, AND TO STRIVE TO BE A WORLD-CHANGER. —B. C.

ACKNOWLEDGMENTS

My primary source for *Barack Obama: Son of Promise, Child of Hope* was the elegantly written Barack Obama memoir, *Dreams from My Father*. As I sought to create an infinitely smaller biography of Obama, I found his writings rich in both information and inspiration. Obviously, this version of Barack Obama's story is compressed and simplified for an audience of young readers. Some artistic license, both in text and visuals, is in operation here. And yet, I have striven to maintain the integrity of *Dreams from My Father*. I'm grateful to Mr. Obama for writing his book.

Thanks also go to editor Alexandra Cooper, who put this ball in my court; to my agent, Elizabeth Harding, who actually believed I could pull this off; and to Kathleen Schoepf, my able research assistant. I'm grateful as well to friends and family who supported me, but I'm especially grateful to children's literature professor Miguel Lopez, my dear friend, for prayerfully holding my hand throughout the course of this whirlwind project.

Thanks to all.

—Nikki Grimes

SIMON & SCHUSTER BOOKS FOR YOUNG READERS · An imprint of Simon & Schuster Children's Publishing Division · 1230 Avenue of the Americas, New York, New York 10020 · Text copyright © 2008 by Nikki Grimes · Illustrations copyright © 2008 by Bryan Collier · All rights reserved, including the right of reproduction in whole or in part in any form. · SIMON & SCHUSTER BOOKS FOR YOUNG READERS is a trademark of Simon & Schuster, Inc. · For information about special discounts for bulk purchases, please contact Simon & Schuster Special Sales at 1-866-506-1949 or business@simonandschuster.com. · The Simon & Schuster Speakers Bureau can bring authors to your live event. For more information or to book an event, contact the Simon & Schuster Speakers Bureau at 1-866-248-3049 or visit our website at www.simonspeakers.com. · Also available in a Simon & Schuster Books for Young Readers hardcover edition · Book design by Lucy Ruth Cummins · The text for this book is set in Tyfa. · The illustrations for this book are rendered in mixed media. · Manufactured in China · 0317 SCP · First Simon & Schuster Books for Young Readers paperback edition January 2012

8   10   9

The Library of Congress has cataloged the hardcover edition as follows: Grimes, Nikki. · Barack Obama: son of promise, child of hope / Nikki Grimes; illustrated by Bryan Collier. — 1st ed. · p. cm. · Includes bibliographical references. · ISBN 978-1-4169-7144-3 (hardcover) · 1. Obama, Barack—Juvenile literature. 2. Legislators—United States—Biography—Juvenile literature. 3. African American legislators—Biography—Juvenile literature. 4. United States. Congress. Senate—Biography—Juvenile literature. 5. Presidential candidates—United States—Biography—Juvenile literature. 6. Racially mixed people—United States—Biography—Juvenile literature. I. Collier, Bryan, ill. II. Title. · E901.1.O23G75 2008 · 328.73092—dc22 · [B] · 2008006245 · ISBN 978-1-4424-4092-0 (pbk) · ISBN 978-1-4169-8464-1 (eBook)